3/31/85

Dear David,

We honor an Einstein readily & without consideration. How often do we honor the Einstein in ourselves?

Please take a moment each day to tell yourself what a perfect pixel you are.

With respect, appreciation & love,

EINSTEIN
A PORTRAIT

With an introduction by Mark Winokur

Pomegranate Artbooks

EINSTEIN: A Portrait
An original publication by Pomegranate Artbooks
Box 980, Corte Madera, California 94925

ISBN 0-917556-97-6

Introduction © 1984 Mark Winokur
Front cover: At Princeton, 1938
            Photograph by Lotte Jacobi ©

Designed by Bonnie Jean Smetts and Suellen Ehnebuske.

Printed in Singapore by Tien Wah Press.

The publisher gratefully acknowledges the generous cooperation of Mr. Ehud Benamy of The American Friends of The Hebrew University.

I want to know how God created this world. I am

not interested in this or that phenomenon, in the

spectrum of this or that element; I want to know his

thoughts; the rest are details.

"Concern for man himself and his fate must always form the chief interest of all technical endeavors.... Never forget this in the midst of your diagrams and equations."

As a myth-making species, humanity tends to simplify—and so render harmless—its conceptions of its great men. We pay an easy homage to the brilliant physicist so that we do not have to understand the public Einstein, who had an enormous and complex effect on modern politics, philosophy, and social reform. The purpose of this collection of photographs and quotations is to reveal a man sometimes condemnatory, sometimes cynical, always critical, but ultimately and realistically hopeful about humanity's ability to survive and thrive in spite of what seems its own worst self-destructive impulses.

This real but limiting awe for Einstein the founder of modern physics is complemented by a love for Einstein the gentle and benevolent old man. This affection, though well-intentioned, obscures the reality of Einstein's activism with a partial truth. The two or three very famous photographs of Einstein show us only an elderly, kind and thoughtful man whose thoughts are not of this world. Everyone has his favorite Einstein story. Friends retell countless tales about his absentmindedness and other-worldiness. On walking home, Einstein would be so wrapped in thought that he would pass his house or lose his way home. Or, while attending a banquet, he was so busy jotting down his thoughts that, not realizing a standing ovation was in his honor, he got up and started clapping, too. Many of these stories are true, but in the telling they erase the memory of a complex public figure and replace it with a myth about an eccentric, private man.

Few people know the Einstein who, partly as a result of the horrors of the first World War, became a world-famous—and often hated—spokesman for pacifism. And not many people remember the Einstein who became so committed to, and identified with, the dream of a separate state for homeless Jews that in 1952 he was offered the presidency of the newly independent state (though one Israeli official responsible for suggesting his nomination stated that if Einstein actually accepted, Israel would be in big trouble). Almost no one recognizes in Einstein the civil libertarian who supported conscientious objection, or the dedicated educationist who helped gather political and economic support for universities and individual scholars.

Even those who are dimly aware of Einstein's status as a spokesman on very controversial issues right up to his death in 1955 (he was, for instance, an early proponent of universal disarmament even in the anxious days of McCarthyism) are rarely aware of the complexity of the man in relation to these issues. For instance, though a pacifist, he believed in the sad necessity of the war against fascism in World War II and never forgave the Germans for the holocaust of the Jews. Einstein tried to maintain a political balance between the desire for individual freedom and the need for universal concordance. He constantly walked a fine line between a belief in an Israeli state as a refuge for homeless Jews and a need for a world organization like the United Nations that would supercede the authority of all individual states in matters of international peace.

In this collection we remember the scientist Einstein because he made possible Einstein the political analyst, social activist and moral philosopher. His powers of rational thought had an enormous impact when applied to his sense of man as a moral and political phenomenon. He used his status as the world's leading physicist as a platform to gain worldwide recognition for his outspoken belief in civil rights and world peace. Finally, the scientist believed that the violence and brutality of many of men's actions violated the beautiful and harmonious laws of nature to which he devoted a lifetime explaining. What to us may seem a utopian vision of the world was for him a truth based on the very real fact of a harmonious nature with whose laws he was intimately familiar.

As a man, the three descriptions that may best sum up his character are realist, bohemian and citizen of the world.

Einstein held citizenship in four countries in the course of his life. As a youth he gave up his citizenship in the Austrian empire for Swiss citizenship, which he held after he became a resident of Germany and a citizen of the United States. But this varied citizenship was only an instance of a larger allegiance to the human community. He practiced this empathy wherever he traveled—Europe, America, South America, Asia, Russia—through a firm outspokenness about the politics of whatever nation in which he resided or visited. He was accessible to all people who came to see him, though the prominent and powerful were often discomfited by the egalitarian instinct that allowed him to treat great and small with equal politeness—but also with equal perception, criticism and penetration. Even close friends noticed in him a universal critical sense that often made it difficult to tell whether his laughter was not directed at their foibles as much as at their jokes.

Einstein's carelessness in dress and his carelessness about social forms were not so much products of absentmindedness as they were results of a lifelong bohemianism. This non-conformity was evident in more practical ways as well. One biographer and friend said that Einstein was the freest man he had ever known. The personal detatchment and aloofness that in part characterized the man also contributed to the freedom of the independent thinker and social reformer. A kind of amused aloofness enabled him to regard with objectivity the failings of an often self-destructive humanity. At one time he asserted that as he grew older, he found it increasingly difficult to distinguish the saner communities from the insane ones.

As a humanist, philosopher and surveyor of the human condition, Einstein was not a visionary optimist who believed unreservedly in the effortless ability of humanity to advance toward a technologically-based utopian society. With the same brilliant synthetic sensibility that struggled to formulate a unified field theory, he maintained as a professional credo a relationship between ethics and moral responsibility, and scientific research. For Einstein, ethics provided the goals for science. While he believed that the state should not place limitations on pure research, he also thought that scientists should direct their own efforts toward those discoveries most beneficial to humanity. Although not religious in any formal sense, he believed that "the finer speculations in the realm of science spring from a deep religious feeling and that without such feeling they would not be fruitful." This sensibility contributed to a sense of moral obligation in the scientist as well.

Einstein easily might have been satisfied with the fame he had garnered as a physicist, content to theorize about humanity from the sidelines. But the philosopher and humanist Einstein would be much less important to us if we did not also have the activist and public reformer Einstein, the actor who had the courage of the theoretician's convictions. Paradoxically, it was in part his carelessness about his fame that made it possible for him to defend controversial issues. He was as indifferent to public notoriety as he was to public acclaim, except insofar as his scientific eminence gave him a platform to polemicize. For over forty years from the beginning of World War I, Einstein was a tireless and outspoken public proponent of all the humanitarian theories he believed in. While he was a good public speaker, his activities included the most practical aspects of social activism. He raised funds for universities and peace movements, wrote articles, corresponded and conversed with major social and political figures, joined and even headed international peace organizations, lent his name and prestige to other organizations and movements, and patronized younger thinkers and writers. Even such personal actions as renouncing his German citizenship became important public statements about his political beliefs.

The list of people with whom Einstein became associated in the course of his public career reads like a *Who's Who* of the socially concerned. From his correspondence with Franklin Roosevelt to his conversation with Charles Chaplin, he remained unabashed in his support of social reform. Einstein maintained a long friendship with the famed French pacifist Romain Rolland. He alternately argued and agreed with the doctrines of Zionist Chaim Weizmann, and he discussed the inequities of the capitalist system with John D. Rockefeller. He argued about the inherent goodness of man with the other great thinker and innovator of the twentieth century, Sigmund Freud. He came to know the great English playwright and Fabian George Barnard Shaw, and he discussed the possibility of the Second World War with Winston Churchill and Lloyd George. In his last years he was close to Bertrand Russell. He knew figures as diverse as Upton Sinclair, Thomas Mann and the King and Queen of Belgium.

As a political thinker and social reformer Einstein was influenced by the works of Tolstoi and the actions of Gandhi. He believed that the reformer's tool of passive resistance, which Gandhi used to attain the independence of India from England, could be applied globally for universal disarmament, a cause for which he fought through most of his life after World War I. His horror of militarism and fascism grew from his experiences in the highly regimented life at the German *gymnasium,* where he attended high school.

The creation and maintenance of a world organization designed specifically to prevent war was Einstein's most durable and important commitment. This organization was to be a universal federation of nations to whose jurisdiction subordinate countries would have to submit in international disputes. It would be the only organization entitled to an army. From his first campaign in 1914 at the outbreak of World War I for a united Europe, through his wary support of the League of Nations and his advocacy of the United Nations, his largest political concern was pacifism and world peace, even though he was critical of the effectiveness of specific organizations. He was not a doctrinaire socialist. Again, his personal unorthodoxy and hatred of regimentation would not allow him to subscribe to any political dogma. But he did not believe that individual countries would disarm voluntarily without the sanction and protection of a larger arbitrating authority. He did not believe in partial disarmament, or disarmament in stages.

Another instance of his public internationalism was his belief that scientists and scholars should be at the forefront of the fight for universal cooperation. Throughout his life he supported the move toward an international freedom in the exchange of research between the scientists of all nationalities. He insisted that such freedom would open the door to other kinds of cultural and political exchanges and would, in turn, promote a sense of universal community for the thinkers and actors of all countries.

Einstein's stand on the importance of scientific freedom was complemented by his sense of the need for the universal accessibility of education. He was instrumental in gaining support for the establishment of at least two prestigious institutions: Brandeis University in the United States, and the Hebrew University in Israel. Once they were founded, he remained active and interested in their policies (he was critical of the Hebrew University's tendency to appoint older, already prominent academics, rather than promising, needy younger scholars) and assisted in finding positions for scientists doing worthwhile research.

Though not observant as a religious Jew, Einstein nevertheless felt a bond of brotherhood with fellow Jews and a sympathy for their plight. He expressed this bond in such activities as finding homes and employment for refugees from Hitler's Germany. Despite — even because of — his eminence as a scientist, Einstein was not immune to anti-semitic slander and attack and was hated particularly in Germany during his residence there between the two World Wars. Both his social activism and his theories in physics were branded as conspiratorially Jewish ways of thinking. These accusations were brought against him even by other — Aryan — physicists.

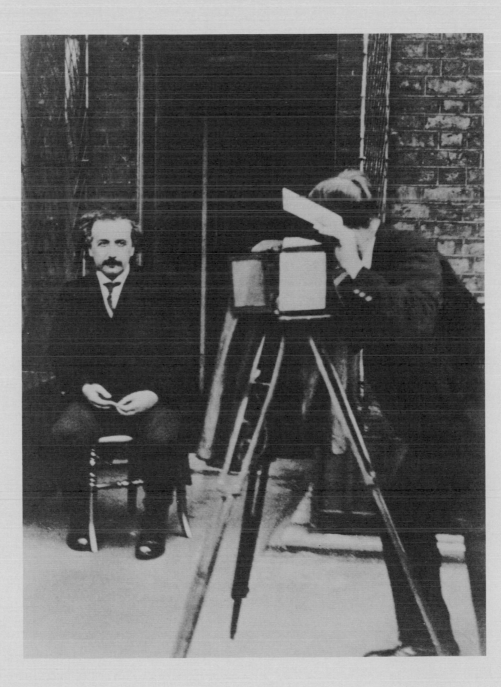

15

I am truly a 'lone traveler' and have never belonged

to my country, my home, my friends, or even my

immediate family, with my whole heart; in the face

of all these ties, I have never lost a sense of distance

and a need for solitude—feelings which increase

with the years.

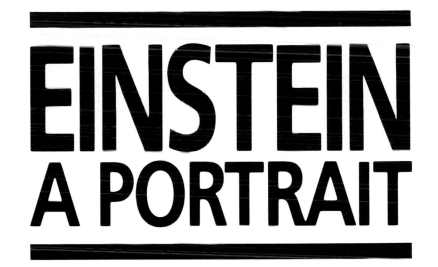

EINSTEIN
A PORTRAIT

O *Youth: Do you know that yours is not the first*

generation to yearn for a life full of beauty and

freedom? Do you know that all your ancestors felt

as you do—and fell victim to trouble and hatred?

21

In living through this "great epoch" it is difficult to

reconcile oneself to the fact that one belongs to that

idiotic, rotten species which boasts of its freedom

of will. How I wish that somewhere there existed an

island for those who are wise and of good will!

In such a place even I should be an ardent patriot.

23

We are faced with the dismaying fact that the

politicians, the practical men of affairs, have become

the exponents of international ideas.

25

With fame I become more and more stupid, which,

of course, is a very common phenomenon. There

is far too great a disproportion between what one

is and what others think one is, or at least what

they say they think one is. But one has to take it all

with good humor.

27

Where the world ceases to be the scene of our

personal hopes and wishes, where we face it as free

beings admiring, asking, and observing, there we

enter the realm of Art and Science.

29

How is it possible that this culture-loving era could be so monstrously amoral? More and more I come to value charity and love of one's fellow being above everything else…all our lauded technological progress—our very civilization—is like the axe in the hand of the pathological criminal.

I have never looked upon ease and happiness as ends in themselves—this ethical basis I call the ideal of a pigsty.

33

Force always attracts men of low morality, and

I believe it to be an invariable rule that tyrants of

genius are succeeded by scoundrels.

The man who regards his own life and that of his

fellow creatures as meaningless is not merely unhappy

but hardly fit for life.

One becomes sharply aware, but without regret, of

the limits of mutual understanding and consonance

with other people.

The most beautiful experience we can have is the

mysterious. It is the fundamental emotion which

stands at the cradle of true art and true science....

I am satisfied with the mystery of the eternity of life.

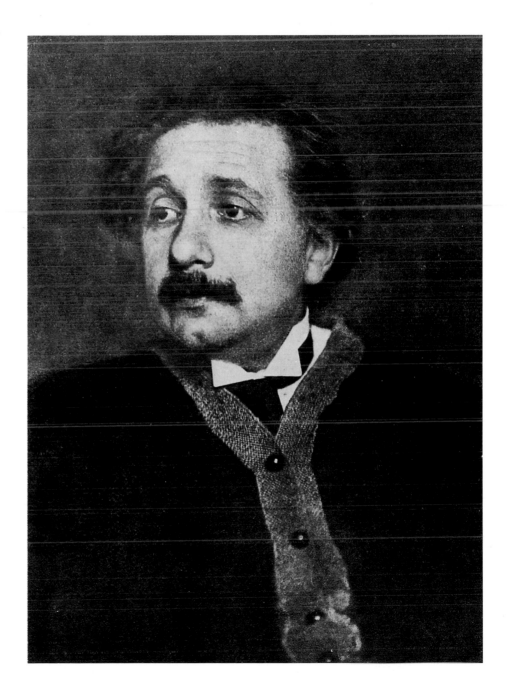

41

One lives all one's life under constant tension until

it is time to go for good.

43

A *hundred times every day I remind myself that my*

inner and outer lives are based on the labors of

other men, living and dead, and that I must exert

myself in order to give in the same measure as I have

received and am still receiving.

45

The true value of a human being is determined

primarily by the measure and the sense in which he

has attained liberation from the self.

47

Do not pride yourself on the few great men who,

over the centuries, have been born on your earth

through no merit of yours. Reflect, rather, on how

you treated them at the time, and how you have

followed their teachings.

Small is the number of them that see with their own

eyes and feel with their own hearts.

51

Philosophy is like a mother who gave birth to and

endowed all the other sciences. Therefore, one

should not scorn her in her nakedness and poverty,

but should hope, rather, that part of her Don Quixote

ideal will live on in her children so that they do not

sink into philistinism.

53

There is, after all, something eternal that lies beyond

reach of the hand of fate and of all human delusions.

And such eternals lie closer to an older person than

to a younger one oscillating between fear and hope.

One misses the elementary reaction against injustice and for justice—that reaction which in the long run represents man's only protection against a relapse into barbarism.

Violence sometimes may have cleared away obstruc-

tions quickly, but it never has proved itself creative.

It is only to the individual that a soul is given.

Perfection of means and confusion of goals seem

to characterize our age. If we desire sincerely and

passionately the safety, the welfare and the free

development of the talents of all men, we shall not

be in want of the means to approach such a state.

Politics is a pendulum whose swings between

anarchy and tyranny are fueled by perennially

rejuvenated illusions.

The ancients knew something which we seem to

have forgotten. All means prove but a blunt instru-

ment, if they have not behind them a living spirit.

57

Einstein to keep that life *private*, to shield something from the opinions and speculations of an adoring but intrusive public audience who otherwise knew every conceivable fact about his public existence.

We tend to equate solitariness with unhappiness in our media-dominated culture. We believe that what we don't know about the life of an eminent person is inaccessible because it is tragic. Why would Einstein otherwise deny complete access to an audience ready to adore his every thought, his every statement? And so we build a mythology about a man who is essentially other-worldly because he is unhappy with this world, when we would be more accurate to observe that Einstein seemed to receive from his closest relations and most private moments the inspirations expressed through his public self. Though it is almost impossible for us to emulate the genius and energy of Einstein, the best lessons we can derive from his life have to do not with creating a mythic figure whose life was lived on a much larger scale than our own, but with emulating a man who was genuinely content only when making his talents accessible to, and useful for, all people in need. We can emulate the humanitarian Einstein who tried to achieve in public life what he achieved in physics: the raising and dignifying of all people to their proper place in the cosmos.

Einstein expressed his commitment to the Jews through a passionate Zionism as well as through his social work and his activities in behalf of the Hebrew University. While he deplored the militancy of many leading Zionist figures, he believed that Jews should have their own homeland, both as a refuge from a long history of discrimination, and as a way of establishing an identity as a unified people with a sense of pride and a distinct voice in world affairs.

His sense of the civil rights of groups of people was extended in several directions. In America, Einstein spoke out in favor of civil rights in the Scottsboro case, in defense of black civil liberties, and in the case of a labor leader unjustly accused of terrorist activities. In Europe, he defended the rights of oppressed minorities, conscientious objectors, and a professor with pacifist politics. He fought for amnesty for political prisoners. The list of activities is almost endless.

For one still convinced of Einstein's naiveté in the political arena it is interesting to examine some of the predictions he made based on his sense of the political currents of his time. Between the two World Wars, Einstein deplored the isolationist policies adopted by America in relation to the increasingly aggressive policies of fascist countries. He foresaw that this policy would ultimately embroil the United States in another world war. He predicted the advent of an increasingly technological military, including the development of the neutron bomb and post-war nuclear proliferation. In the field of Middle Eastern politics, Einstein warned that if the fledgling Israel did not maintain a beneficently neutral attitude toward its Arab neighbors, the resulting tensions would be explosive. Finally, he foresaw that if humanity did not establish some system of nuclear self-regulation, it would become capable of destroying itself. We must wait to see the outcome only of the last prediction.

There is an irony in the fact that a man whose adult life was devoted to public affairs was characterized by his friends as "solitary," "apart," "aloof" and "lonely." While we have to be wary of the tendency to romanticize Einstein as a man who was denied a private life so that he could devote himself more completely to public works, it is hard to discount the reports of so many acquaintances and friends. The truth seems to be that despite a circle of close friends and family, Einstein did remain in some ways solitary. But this inaccessibility to some private self was a conscious act of decision, similar to his refusal to be impressed by his own fame. In order to have any private life it was necessary for

One can organize to apply a discovery already made,

but not to make one.

It is a mistake often made in this country to measure

things by the amount of money they cost.

The real difficulty, the difficulty that has baffled the

sages of all times, is rather this: how can we make

our teaching so potent in the emotional life of man,

that its influence should withstand the pressure of

the elemental psychic forces in the individual?

This is what I have to say about Bach's life work:

listen, play, love, revere—and keep your mouth shut.

All of us who are concerned for peace and the

triumph of reason and justice must be keenly aware

how small an influence reason and honest good will

exert upon events in the political field.

It is best, it seems to me, to separate one's inner

striving from one's trade as far as possible. It is

not good when one's daily bread is tied to God's

special blessing.

Do not worry about your difficulties in mathematics;

I can assure you that mine are still greater.

It is really a puzzle what drives one to take one's

work so devilishly seriously. For whom? For oneself?

One soon leaves, after all. For one's contemporaries?

For posterity? No, it remains a puzzle.

The unlimited desire for ever greater power seeks to become active and aggressive wherever and whenever the physical possibility offers itself.

External compulsion can, to a certain extent, reduce

but never cancel the responsibility of the individual.

Democratic institutions and standards are the result of historic developments to an extent not always appreciated in the lands which enjoy them.

It is characteristic of the military mentality that non-

human factors are held essential, while the human

being—his desires and thoughts are considered as

unimportant and secondary.

The most important human endeavor is the striving

for morality in our actions. Our inner balance and

even our very existence depend on it. Only morality

in our actions can give beauty and dignity to life.

Whoever undertakes to set himself up as judge in

the field of Truth and Knowledge is shipwrecked by

the laughter of the gods.

I do not believe in immortality of the individual, and

I consider ethics to be an exclusively human concern

with no superhuman authority behind it.

The deeper we penetrate and the more extensive and embracing our theories become, the less empirical knowledge is needed to determine those theories.

One is born into a herd of buffaloes and must be

glad if one is not trampled underfoot before

one's time.

Few people are capable of expressing with equa-

nimity opinions which differ from the prejudices of

their social environment. Most people are even

incapable of forming such opinions.

In Faraday's day there did not yet exist the dull

specialization that stares with self-conceit through

hornrimmed glasses and destroys poetry.

What a person thinks on his own, without being

stimulated by the thoughts and experiences of

other people, is even in the best case rather paltry

and monotonous.

Paula Wright

It may affront the military-minded person to suggest

a regime that does not maintain any military secrets.

In order to be an immaculate member of a flock of

sheep, one must above all be a sheep oneself.

The existence and validity of human rights are not

written in the stars.

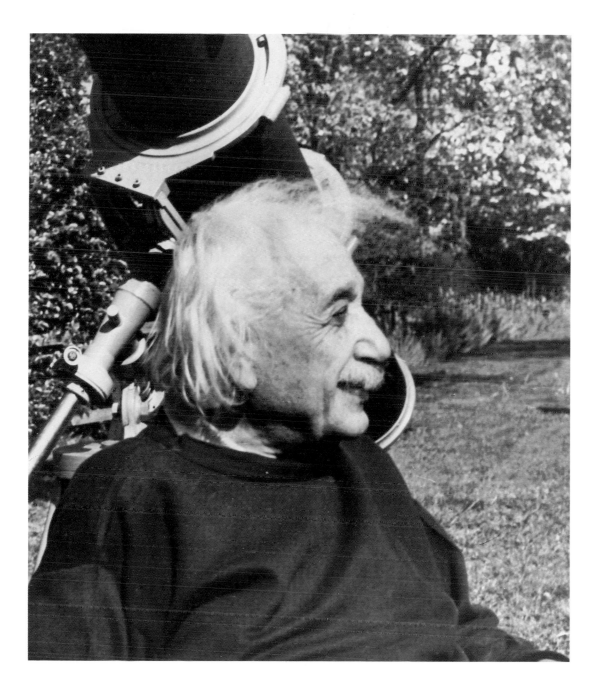

A *man must learn to understand the motives of*

human beings, their illusions, and their sufferings.

One has been endowed with just enough intelligence

to be able to see clearly how utterly inadequate that

intelligence is when confronted with what exists.

If such humility could be conveyed to everybody, the

world of human activities would be more appealing.

Is there not a certain satisfaction in the fact that

natural limits are set to the life of the individual, so

that at its conclusion it may appear as a work of art?

Sources and Credits:

Quotations

pg. 7, From the article "A Talk with Finstein," published in *The Listener,* September, 1955

pg. 17, From the Forum series *Living Philosophies, ca. 1930*

pg. 20, From a letter to a daughter of a friend, Caputh, 1932

pg. 22, From a letter to Paul Ehrenfest, Berlin, December, 1914

pg. 24, Written after the creation of the League of Nations, ca. 1919

pg. 26, From a letter to Heinrich Zangger, 1919

pg. 28, From a magazine article on modern art, 1921

pg. 30, From a letter to Heinrich Zangger, Berlin, December, 1917

pg. 32, From the Forum series *Living Philosophies, ca. 1930*

pg. 34, From the Forum series *Living Philosophies, ca. 1930*

pg. 36, From *The World As I See It,* 1931

pg. 38, From the Forum series *Living Philosophies, ca. 1930*

pg. 40, From the Forum series *Living Philosophies, ca. 1930*

pg. 42, From a letter to his sister, Maja, 1935

pg. 44, From *The World As I See It,* 1931

pg. 46, From *The World As I See It,* 1931

Photographs

pg. 15, England, ca. early 1920's, courtesy Historical Picture Service, Chicago

pg. 21, Zurich ca. 1900, photograph given to Lotte Jacobi by Einstein for reproduction rights; courtesy Lotte Jacobi © (LJAIO)

pg. 23, Bern, Switzerland ca. 1905, photograph given to Lotte Jacobi by Einstein for reproduction rights; courtesy Lotte Jacobi © (LJA1)

pg. 25, Germany, 1917, photograph by S. Byk; courtesy of Black Star © 1984

pg. 27, Berlin, ca. 1915–1920, courtesy of the Bettmann Archive (A33)

pg. 29, Berlin, 1921, courtesy of Ullstein Bilderdienst (B83)

pg. 31, Leiden, Netherlands, 1923, photograph by Gerhard H. Dieke, © The Hebrew University of Jerusalem, courtesy American Institute of Physics, Niels Bohr Library (B25)

pg. 33, Berlin, ca. early 1920's, photograph by Sigismund Jacobi, courtesy Lotte Jacobi © (A7)

pg. 35, Berlin, ca. 1922, courtesy The Bettmann Archive (B56)

pg. 37, Berlin, 1922, courtesy of Ullstein Bilderdienst (B85)

pg. 39, Germany, ca. early 1920's, photograph by Schloss; courtesy of American Institute of Physics, Niels Bohr Library (A3)

Sources and Credits:

Quotations

pg. 48, From Einstein's private papers; occasion unknown, probably Pasadena, 1932–1933

pg. 50, From *The World As I See It,* 1931

pg. 52, From a letter to a correspondent, 1932

pg. 54, From a letter to Queen Elizabeth of Belgium, 1936

pg. 56, From a message to the Young Men's Christian Association, 1937

pg. 58, From an address at the Princeton Theological Seminary, 1939

pg. 60, From *"Was Europe a Success?",The Nation,* New York, October 3,1934

pg. 62, From an address at the Princeton Theological Seminary, 1939

pg. 64, From a broadcast recording for the Science Conference, London, 1941

pg. 66, Written at Huntington, New York, 1937

pg. 68, From the *Atlantic Monthly,* 1945

pg. 70, From the *Atlantic Monthly,* 1945

pg. 72, From an address at Swarthmore College, 1938

Photographs

pg. 41, Berlin, ca. mid-1920's, engraving by Rose Weiser, Photographische Gesellschaft; courtesy American Institute of Physics, Niels Bohr Library (A14)

pg. 43, Berlin, 1927, courtesy of Ullstein Bilderdienst (B86)

pg. 45, Berlin, 1930, courtesy of Ullstein Bilderdienst (B87)

pg. 47, Caputh, Germany, 1930, photography by H. Landshoff ©, courtesy American Institute of Physics, Niels Bohr Library (B18)

pg. 49, Oxford, England, 1931, courtesy Brown Brothers (A22)

pg. 51, Pasadena, California, 1932, photograph by E. Willard Spurr, courtesy Library of Congress.

pg. 53, Pasadena, California, 1932, courtesy California Institute of Technology Archives (B74)

pg. 55, Pasadena, California ca. 1930–1933, courtesy Brown Brothers (B32)

pg. 57, ca. 1930–1932, photograph by Johan Hagemeyer, Bancroft Library, courtesy American Institute of Physics, Niels Bohr Library (B15)

pg. 59, Berlin, 1934, courtesy The Bettmann Archive (B57)

pg. 61, 1935, courtesy of Library of Congress

Quotations

Photographs

Sources and Credits:

Quotations

pg. 104, From a letter to Gertrud Warschauer, 1952

pg. 106, From an article written for *Jungkaufmann,* 1952

pg. 108, From the *Atlantic Monthly,* 1947

pg. 110, From a commemorative in honor of Leo Baeck, 1953

pg. 112, From an address to the Chicago Decalogue Society, 1954

pg. 114, From the *New York Times,* 1952

pg. 116, From a letter to Queen Elizabeth of Belgium, 1932

pg. 118, From *La Pensee,* Paris, February-March, 1947

Photographs

pg. 89, ca. 1947–1950, photograph by Albert Fenn, courtesy Life Magazine, © Time, Inc.

pg. 91, 1948, courtesy Culver Pictures, Inc. (A37)

pg. 93, Princeton, 1948, photograph by Alfred Eisenstaedt, courtesy Life Magazine, © 1948 Time Inc. (B101)

pg. 95, Princeton, 1949, courtesy Brown Brothers (B41)

pg. 97, 1949, courtesy Culver Pictures, Inc. (B71)

pg. 99, Princeton, ca. 1950, photograph by Alan Richards, © Institute for Advanced Study (B80)

pg. 101, 1950, photograph by Doreen Spooner, courtesy Keystone Press Agency, Inc. (B14)

pg. 103, Princeton, 1951, photograph by Ernst Haas, © 1970 Magnum Photos (B53)

pg. 105, Princeton, 1951, photograph by Ernst Haas, courtesy © Magnum Photos, Inc. (B54)

pg. 107, Princeton, ca. early 1950's, photograph by Paula Wright, courtesy Black Star (A44)

pg. 109, ca. 1950, courtesy American Institute of Physics, Niels Bohr Library, photograph by Ulli Steltzer (B28)

pg. 111, Princeton, ca. 1953–1954, courtesy American Institute of Physics, Niels Bohr Library (B22)

Photographs

pg. 113, Princeton, 1954, courtesy American Institute of Physics, Niels Bohr Library, Gezari Collection (B6)

pg. 115, Princeton, 1954, courtesy American Institute of Physics, Niels Bohr Library, Gezari Collection (B3)

pg. 117, 1955, courtesy Brown Brothers (B33)

pg. 119, Princeton, 1954, photograph by Sanford Roth, © Beulah Roth

pg. 121, Princeton, 1954, photograph by Sanford Roth, © Beulah Roth